MYSTERIES OF CRYPTOCURRENCY

FROM AN ORDINARY WORKING STIFF   BY JAMES AND DOROTHY SANNES

I0513144

MYSTERIES OF CRYPTOCURRENCY

FROM AN ORDINARY WORKING STIFF

By

James and Dorothy Sannes

This Book was written for pure enjoyment and fun and profit.

Copyright 2018, James L. & Dorothy Sannes
All rights reserved.
No part of this book may be reproduced, stored in a retrieval system,
Or transmitted by any means, electronic, mechanical, photocopying, recording, or otherwise, without written permission from the author.

MYSTERIES OF CRYPTOCURRENCY

FROM AN ORDINARY WORKING STIFF   BY JAMES AND DOROTHY SANNES

Look for our other books

"Ice Tea and Roses" A mystery, and its sequel, Deadly Insights,

Nightmares of a Step Daughter,

Gentle Moments, Notes from the Lord

Simple Things You Can Do To Carry Your Child Through School,

Favorite Recipes From the Hearts of our Family,

The Treasure of Anasazi Indians,

Beyond Roswell I "We are Definitely Not Alone,

Beyond Roswell II The Hidden Truth,

After Eden Beyond Roswell III Beyond Roswell, Hidden Valley Second Chance and Wise Old Man's Betting Tips

Now available in www.amazon.com

MYSTERIES OF CRYPTOCURRENCY

FROM AN ORDINARY WORKING STIFF   BY JAMES AND DOROTHY SANNES

About Me, the Author

Like most authors in most of other books that are for sale.

I'm just a regular person like anyone else so I don't have a fancy title, I'm just an everyday working stiff trying to make a living for my family.

I do love working with numbers and playing with anything that has odds, and I do believe in CRYPTOCURRENCY as being the future of the world currency.

As I'm enjoying the work I'm doing, studying the future of this currency I want you to enjoy reading this book because it was fun to write.

Jim Sannes

MYSTERIES OF CRYPTOCURRENCY

FROM AN ORDINARY WORKING STIFF   BY JAMES AND DOROTHY SANNES

Introduction;

This is how I started out, I was thinking the gold bitcoins that I saw on Amazon were the real thing.

I even went so far as buying several of them because they were beautiful. They look nice setting on my desk, unknown to me, some were plastic and worthless but again they were beautiful.

Then I bought some books on Amazon thinking they would help, they have lots of words but little help.

But, I dove right in and started studying them more and more every day.

MYSTERIES OF CRYPTOCURRENCY

FROM AN ORDINARY WORKING STIFF   BY JAMES AND DOROTHY SANNES

Chapter One

"Basics of Cryptocurrency"

It is digital currency not coins, like I thought. You can't hold it in your hands as I first thought. Like I said I bought some very beautiful ones that I now have on my desk, I love looking at them.

I found out I needed to check into what they called Coinbase, it's a cryptocurrency platform. So, I needed to send some of my fun money that I would be using to Coinbase to get started.

Chapter Two

I still don't know anyone that is into bitcoins, I've checked with people in my church, around where I work and I struck out, no help anywhere.

So, I got an idea, I ordered some hats on Amazon with the word "bitcoins" in big letters and started wearing it around where ever I went. This seemed to help because slowly people started asking about bitcoin or just saying they were starting to get into it themselves.

The hats were working, I've been meeting people everywhere with the same hopes that the phenomena of bitcoin were really out there. They are having fun with the learning the ins and outs of the game of cryptocurrency just like me.

There is so much information out there, but still so may con artist that will lead you down the wrong path and trying to sell their worthless coins from all over the world. Please check other countries that are selling their coins that they are making up, a lot of them are going into bankrupt in hopes to make money on their worthless coins and leaving us bankrupt instead. like Venezuela just came out with their own coin. Their coin is a RED flag to me.

Believe it or not, there are over 1200 different coins out there, so make sure you check out every coin you wish to put money on.

There is a list I use on Coindex, that shows the values list of todays coins from number one through 1000 or more. So please check out the coins before buying anything.

When investing only invest money you CAN afford to lose. I pray that won't happen, but coins are very volatile, I found I need to hang in there every day. (It's like buying stock).

Coins are always swing up and down in price, but a lot of people are making lots of money on price changes, buying low and selling high. It goes back and forth, and takes a lot of studying. That is what is fun for me, the studying.

And buying low and selling high is how to really cash in.

Chapter Three

"Rise of Cryptocurrencies"

One good thing about Bitcoins are their prices, they are running and changing around the world 24/7 seven days a week. It never stops, on and on night and day, they don't shut down like a local bank would do. Making money goes on 24/7.

I've checked a lot of coin bases to find out what is best for my money. I chose Coinbase to start with, remember to check and read like I did. I came up with Coinbase to be the safest virtual coin base for my money to start. Right now, I like it the best.

Everyone needs to have virtual bank to start as a base and I like Coinbase, but there are lots of other good coinbase banks to help you so do your research and studying and join the one that works for you.

There's more than 1200 cryptocurrencies and the marked caps are approximately 175 billion coins in circulation in the market.

In 2009 Bitcoin was the first cryptocurrency to prove decentralized currency could exist and change the way the world currency will change our future. It shows the world is hungry for change. Our world finances and our governments are fighting cryptocurrency every inch of the way.

They are so afraid to lose power over everyone it is driving the world leaders nuts.

Chapter Four

"Starting With Coinbase"

I was so fired up with just reading all the news, and checking what people like us thinking of becoming rich over night at first it was exciting.

But, first I looked and looked for the best way to start and do it safely. I checked out many different coin bases and I decided on Coinbase as my virtual bank.

It took some time for me to figure out how to join but I followed the instructions and found out that I had to add a picture of myself and inter my regular bank information. I must admit it took me some time to figure all these things out that I needed for the process. I'm 75 years young and not as good on the computer as the younger kids, like my grandsons.

But, thank goodness my wife of 54 years is also good at doing a lot on the computer and we work shoulder to shoulder and we just plug on with what we need to do. We are both very excited with joining what we believe with all our hearts is the future for all of us.

It will be great to get our own government off our backs a little, but no one knows how long it will take. They want every penny they can squeeze out of us.

But finally, I'm in Coinbase, you can put credit cards or money but debit cards work the fastest. Regular credit cards can take up to 5 days to clear.

In order to put your money in, you need to put it into one of the 4 in Bitcoins they have, Bitcoin, Bitcoin Cash, Ethereum, or Litecoin.

You can buy anyone you wish and you can buy 25%, 50%, 75%, or 100% of any one of these coins you wish, it depends on the money you have to invest or just have fun with.

Please check out the biggest Bitcoin exchanges, I believe them to be the safest and best that's why I choose Coinbase as my bank to store my money and to keep down the fees, when buying and trading coins.

You must remember if you choose exchanges over seas you may have to wire your money if you want to buy, and that takes longer to do trades, and some of our local banks may reject our transfers.

Most experts say we should seek an exchange that suits our individual needs, some for example serve sophisticated investors with easy systems for limit and stop-limit orders, but ordinary investors like myself just like to place market orders. Like Coinbase only lets me buy up to $100.00 a week. But you can ask for higher limits the farther you go along.

Chapter Five

I choose Binance for my main exchanges because they have a lot of coins, most people call coins, tokens. I still call mine coins, makes me feel better, and my desk has a lot of beautiful coins displayed there for my excitement, which gives me a good feeling.

Well, Binance I love their charts, which are easy to use. They are great for selling and buying a lot of coins with really fast service which is super important.

They offer other programs of interest also, such as Binance News, Referral information, and a group called Angels.

But it all starts with your account with Coinbase, you need to have your moneys invested in tokens or coins already before doing anything in Binance.

Once you have bought one of these, Bitcoin, Bitcoin Cash, Ethereum, or Litecoin with your money in Coinbase you can just transfer these coins to Binance from Coinbase. It is a very simple process but, Binance has all the information to help you. You have to click on Deposit and find the one you chose from Bitcoin, Bitcoin Cash, Ethereum, or Litecoin and get a code to put into the Coinbase to withdraw then hit withdraw there in Coinbase and it will send it to Binance. Then you need to sell on Binance to buy the one coin you want.

Then once you have your monies in Binance that is when you can choose one of the Tokens or Coins to invest in.

But be very careful, there are so many bad coins out there. You must check out the ones you are interested in, that is what I'm always doing. Look them up on line to find information about the ones that you think look good.

And with Binance they do have really great graphs to let you check on all the coins showing each coin's movements, as well as their percentage changes.

And this is how to make the most of your coins buy know and sale high, but always be careful and do your studying.

BLOCKCHAIN

This is what brings all your coins and all your selling and coin buying together, it is a personal record, but they only exist in the digital world when you buy anything online. You'll be able to use your Cryptocurrencies to get whatever your buying as long as you have plenty of coins to pay the price that is needed.

Blockchain is like they say about Las Vegas, what's in your blockchain *stays* in your blockchain, it's a nice little twist of the tongue. Just remember to have fun with your studying and buying. Be safe, Live Large!

One of my favorite coins is Ripple and has a real company that has a job it can do. It makes me feel safer when the coins have a real function, so be careful with all the coins and don't put more into it than you can afford and would put you into bankruptcy. So please read and do your homework.

I hope you're finding my book helpful for I did have a really good time getting started, like I said I'm just a working stiff trying to have fun with all this, and hopefully make a lot of money like so many regular people have been doing.

Remember there is so much volatility in all the coins, you can still make a lot of money on coins (or tokens as they are calling them now) as they move up and down.

Some have track records to watch but, be careful, I cannot say it enough, do your homework. I was having trouble with boredom sorry to say, maybe because my children are grown and gone, it's just my wife and I, this helps fill that empty void I feel at times.

But, I firmly believe Cryptocurrency is our future, I pray to God people start loving each other, that is and I think our down fall, if not.

Thank you very much for buying and reading my book. Much luck.

Jim and Dorothy

MYSTERIES OF CRYPTOCURRENCY

FROM AN ORDINARY WORKING STIFF   BY JAMES AND DOROTHY SANNES

MYSTERIES OF CRYPTOCURRENCY

FROM AN ORDINARY WORKING STIFF   BY JAMES AND DOROTHY SANNES

www.ingramcontent.com/pod-product-compliance
Lightning Source LLC
Chambersburg PA
CBHW051533240526
45471CB00019B/1340